Kids
Can
Code

Understanding Coding with

MINECRAFT™

Patricia Harris

PowerKiDS
press™

New York

Published in 2016 by The Rosen Publishing Group, Inc.
29 East 21st Street, New York, NY 10010

First Edition

Editor: Greg Roza
Book Design: Michael J. Flynn

Photo Credits: Cover Hero Images/Getty Images; cover, pp. 3–24 (coding background) Lukas Rs/Shutterstock.com; pp. 5, 17 Chris Ratcliffe/Bloomberg/Getty Images; p. 7 Chuck Berman/Chicago Tribune/Tribune News Service/Getty Images; pp. 9–11, 19 (Minecraft screenshots and artwork) Minecraft ®/TM & © 2009–2013 Mojang/Notch; pp. 12–13, 18 (light bulb) Kraska/Shutterstock.com; p. 15 Dragon Images/Shutterstock.com; p. 16 Alexey Rotanov/Shutterstock.com; p. 20 Bloomua/Shutterstock.com.

Minecraft is a trademark of Mojang (a game development studio owned by Microsoft Technology Corporation), and its use in this book does not imply a recommendation or endorsement of this title by Mojang or Microsoft.

Library of Congress Cataloging-in-Publication Data

Harris, Patricia Green, 1942-
 Understanding coding with Minecraft / Patricia Harris.
     pages cm. — (Kids can code)
 Includes index.
 ISBN 978-1-5081-4470-0 (pbk.)
 ISBN 978-1-5081-4471-7 (6 pack)
 ISBN 978-1-5081-4472-4 (library binding)
 1. Computer games—Programming—Juvenile literature. 2. Minecraft (Game)—Juvenile literature. 3. Computer simulation—Juvenile literature. 4. Computers and children—Juvenile literature. I. Title.
 QA76.76.C672H37326 2016
 794.8'1526—dc23
                                    2015034434

Manufactured in the United States of America

CPSIA Compliance Information: Batch #BW16PK: For Further Information contact Rosen Publishing, New York, New York at 1-800-237-9932

Contents

Coding with Cubes

You've probably heard of Minecraft. Maybe you've even explored the giant worlds created by the popular game. Minecraft can be played several different ways. Users can play in "survival **mode**" by gathering **resources** to create buildings, find food, and complete tasks without dying. Or users can play in "creative mode," which allows them to fly around and build whatever they want with all the resources available in the game.

Minecraft provides you with many different blocks and tools to let you build your own world! However, that world is also filled with crazy demons and monsters, secret locations, and underground treasures. Players can spend hours constructing buildings, battling dreaded "creepers," and digging for gems. What many people don't realize is that Minecraft can be used to understand coding.

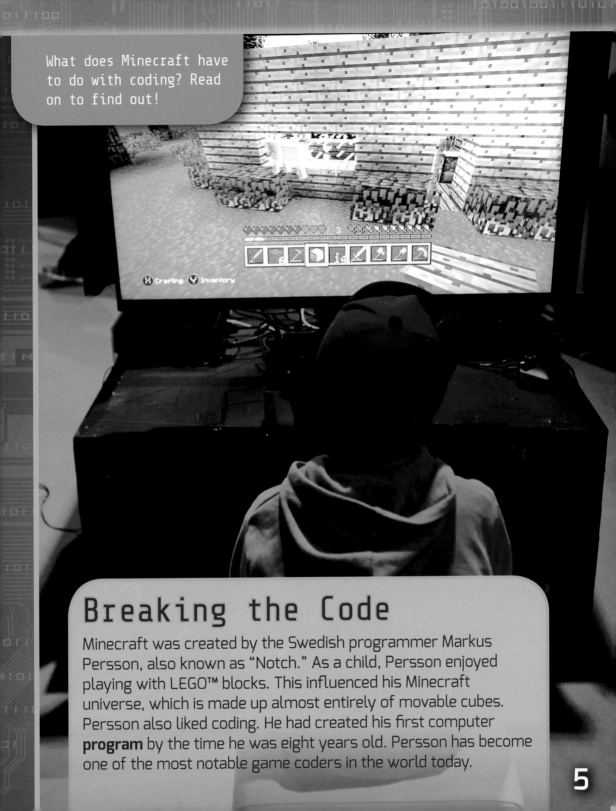

What does Minecraft have to do with coding? Read on to find out!

Breaking the Code

Minecraft was created by the Swedish programmer Markus Persson, also known as "Notch." As a child, Persson enjoyed playing with LEGO™ blocks. This influenced his Minecraft universe, which is made up almost entirely of movable cubes. Persson also liked coding. He had created his first computer **program** by the time he was eight years old. Persson has become one of the most notable game coders in the world today.

Messing Around with Redstone

Minecraft gives gamers many resources to experiment with. Different elements can be combined to make supplies and tools. Games often start with players chopping down trees in order to get wood to build houses. The game contains many other resources, from bricks and glass to weapons and potions.

In 2010, the makers of Minecraft added a new type of resource called Redstone. This can be obtained by mining, combining certain ingredients, or killing witches. Redstone objects include blocks, dust, switches, buttons, and torches. Redstone can be used to brew potions and craft tools. However, this very important resource can also be used to make **circuits**, similar to electrical circuits. Creating Redstone circuits allows users to make moving devices and machines. It also helps users understand the **logic** used to code computer programs.

Coding may sound like something only scientists can do. However, it's not as hard as you might think, especially when using Minecraft to learn about coding.

Breaking the Code

Redstone blocks transmit power just like electrical wires. Players make a circuit using Redstone blocks and other objects, such as doors and switches. If a player doesn't understand how these parts work together, they'll have a hard time making them work properly. When a player understands the logic behind Redstone, they can make some very interesting devices—sensors, locks, lamps, block dispensers, railways, and whatever else young coders can dream up!

Five Rules

Using Minecraft Redstone to create devices can be thought of as using a **programming language**. In order to use any programming language, including Redstone blocks, you need to know that coders must follow certain rules. Rules ensure your coding efforts meet with success no matter what language you're working with.

Rule 1: Coders must know what they want the computer to do and write a plan.

Rule 2: Coders must use special words to have the computer take **input**, make choices, and take action.

Rule 3: Coders need to think about what tasks can be put into a group.

Rule 4: Coders need to use logic with AND, OR, NOT, and other logic statements as key words.

Rule 5: Coders must explore the **environment** and understand how it works.

These pictures show Redstone power at work. The first one shows the end of the track without power. It has black rails because the power is off. The second picture shows the switch turned on, so the track now has power. Imagine all the things you can do with Redstone!

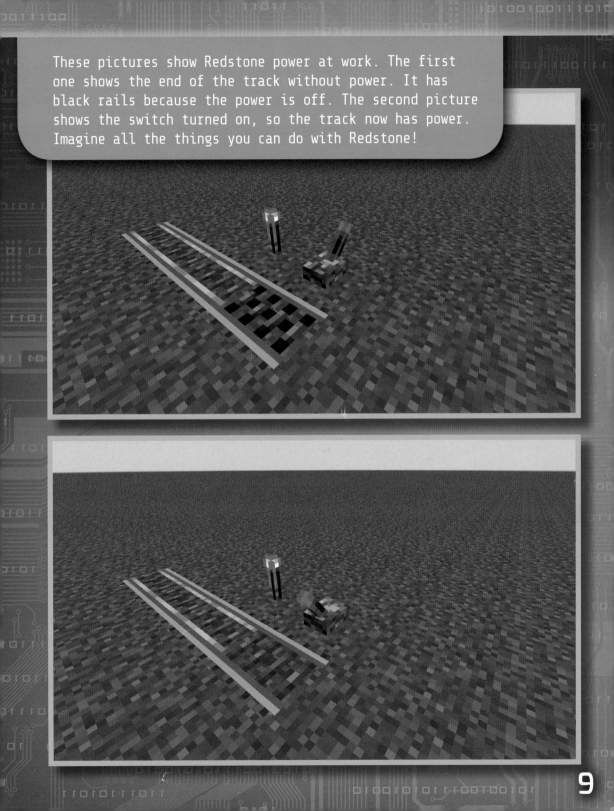

Without Logic

Redstone can do many things in Minecraft. A simple switch can open a door in a house. The switch can be on the wall next to the door. If the switch is away from the door, Redstone dust is used to connect them. This example doesn't require logic.

In this example, Redstone is used to power a railcar from a distance. A button is different from a switch because it just sends power for a moment. Most of the track is powered (red), except for the last piece (black). When the cart arrives at the end, it stops. If you want to bring the cart back, hit the button! The button and trail of Redstone dust send power to the last piece of track. This causes the cart to return to the beginning.

This is just the start of plans for a much larger rail system. You can also add logic gates to your track. Logic gates can make your Minecraft creations more useful and exciting.

Let's Get Logical

The logic of Minecraft coding is established using simple AND, NOT, and other logic "gates." Gates are connections that let information pass from one **component** to another in different ways. Knowing the different gates allows players to make some really amazing devices.

Consider the word "and" in the following sentence: "Tom and Mary like Minecraft." The word "and" joins the two people. Similarly, the AND gate in Minecraft joins two switches. Both switches must be turned on for the connection to work.

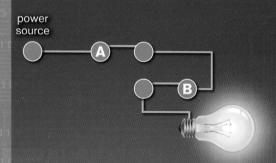

A switch closed (on)
B switch closed (on)

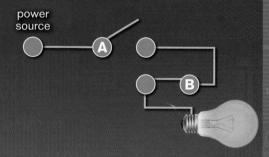

A switch open (off)
B switch closed (on)

This is an example of an AND gate circuit with two switches. The light only works when both switches are closed.

Breaking the Code

While Minecraft is a game, it can let you begin to understand how computers use logic when they work. After all, computers just use switches, or gates, to do all the marvelous things they do.

Here is a new sentence: "Tom does not like Minecraft." In this sentence, "not" joins the person with the action in a negative way. With a NOT gate circuit, the power is on when the switch is open, or off.

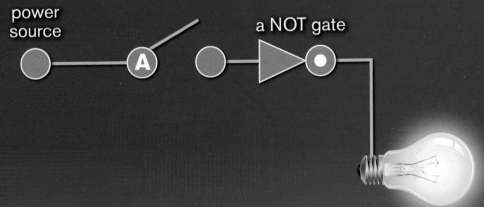

power source

a NOT gate

A switch open (off)

A NOT gate is an **inverter**. It changes how a switch works. An on switch becomes an off switch, and an off switch becomes an on switch. Other Redstone gates include NAND, OR, NOR, XOR, XNOR. Turn to page 22 for more information.

Build and Test

To use logic in Minecraft, you must understand the environment in which Redstone works. Survival mode allows you to test yourself against whatever challenges the world presents. In creative mode, you are free to build a world without challenges.

You should build and test your Redstone devices in the creative mode. That is what good programmers do! They plan their designs and construct them within a controlled environment. They test them to be sure the system works as they expect. Then they use them in the real world.

Programs, however, may not be perfect. When code is used in the real world, problems may come up. The real world often does things we don't expect! Programmers get feedback from the real world and change their designs to work better.

15

Get Connected

To use Redstone, you need to know about Redstone blocks and Redstone dust. Blocks can be crafted from Redstone ore. Think of the blocks as a power source—like a battery in a flashlight. Redstone dust is just Redstone blocks placed on the ground. Think of the dust as electrical wires. Thinking about real-world devices will help you understand how Redstone devices work. For example, a flashlight needs an on/off switch, or else your batteries won't last too long.

Think about the light in a room. The switch is on the wall, but the light is on the ceiling. Think how hard it would be to have the light on if you had to climb up and touch a switch next to the light. In coding—as in electrical work—making connections is important.

In creative mode, players have access to all the game's resources. This makes planning and experimenting simple.

Tools, Weapons & Armour

Leather Pants

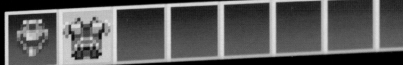

Clear Quick Select   What's This?

Let's say you're in a room with one overhead light and two switches, one next to each door. This circuit requires an OR gate. When either of the switches is on, the light will be on. If both switches are off, the light will be off.

Right now the light is off. However, flipping either switch will complete the circuit and turn the light on.

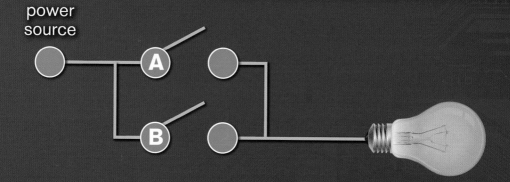

power source

both switches open (off)

Breaking the Code

AND is a logic **construct** that appears in life. You can go to the movies if you have free time AND money for a ticket. Just one of those is not enough. OR logic works in life, too. If you have only a little free time and just enough money, you can either go to the movies OR go bowling. You won't have time or money for both.

You can use an OR gate to power a light in Minecraft. You need a power source, a glowstone for a lamp, Redstone dust, and two switches. You can use a house you've built and add the lights and a switch by each door. Remember to work in creative mode to construct your device. If your dust lines are more than 15 blocks long, you will need to add a repeater block. Redstone dust runs out of power after 15 blocks, so a repeater reinforces the power.

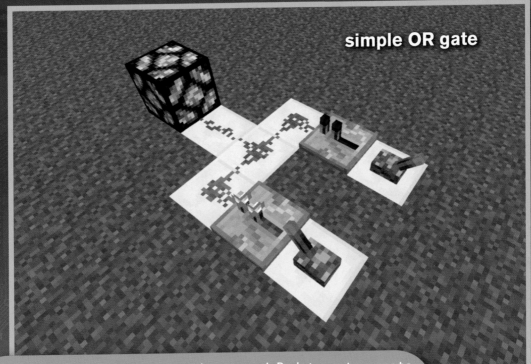

simple OR gate

Expert Minecraft players have used Redstone to create some truly amazing devices—including a 3D printer and even a computer that can process math problems! With Redstone, the sky is the limit.

Open the Gates!

AND, OR, and NOT gates are the simplest gates in Minecraft. Once you've experimented with them, you can move on to more complex gates. On page 21 is a list of the most useful gates in Minecraft. With them, you can make some really amazing devices. These are all based on switch/lamp applications. The diagrams on page 22 show what these gates look like in the game.

So what would you build in Minecraft? Simple light switches are the first step. There's so much more you can do with Redstone when you understand the logic behind it. Once you become an experienced Minecraft coder, you can apply your new programming skills to other computer languages, such as Ruby and Python. Minecraft proves that coding isn't just for scientists—it's for you, too!

AND GATE
The lamp is on if all the switches are on.

OR GATE
The lamp is on if at least one switch is on.

NOT GATE
The lamp is on if the switch is off, and the lamp is off if the switch is on. Known as an inverter.

NAND GATE
The lamp is off when both switches are on. Otherwise, the lamp is on.

NOR GATE
The lamp is off when at least one switch is on. The lamp is on when all switches are off.

XOR GATE
The lamp is on if the switches are opposites from each other. The lamp is off if both switches are on or both are off.

XNOR GATE
The lamp is on if both switches are on or off. The lamp is off if one switch is on and one is off.

COMMON MINECRAFT GATES

air (nothing)	switch (input)	block (generic)	torch (side of block)	torch (top of block)	Redstone (on ground)	Redstone (top of block)	Redstone (output)

NOT GATE

OR GATE

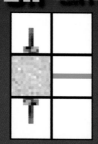

NAND GATE

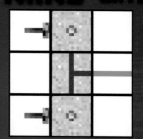

AND GATE

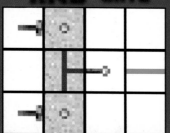

XOR GATE

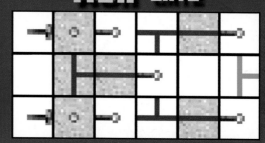

NOR GATE

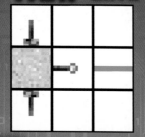

XNOR GATE

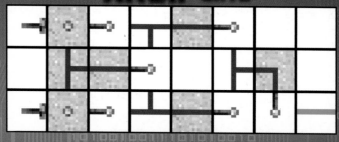

Glossary

circuit: A closed path made of wires or other parts that allows energy or electricity to pass through it.

component: One of the parts of something.

construct: An idea put together, or constructed, by the mind and not in the real world.

environment: The combination of computer hardware and software that allows a user to perform various tasks.

input: Information that is entered into a computer.

inverter: Something that causes something else to work in the opposite way it usually acts.

logic: A proper or reasonable way of thinking about or understanding something.

mode: A form of something that is different from other forms of the same thing.

program: A set of code that runs on a computer and performs certain tasks. Also called software.

programming language: A computer language designed to give instructions to a computer.

resource: A usable supply of something.

Index

Websites

Due to the changing nature of Internet links, PowerKids Press has developed an online list of websites related to the subject of this book. This site is updated regularly. Please use this link to access the list: www.powerkidslinks.com/kcc/mine

7